CATHEDRAL
6·27·83

for Rosemary

best Gothic wishes,

Raymond Carver

HOUGHTON MIFFLIN COMPANY BOSTON

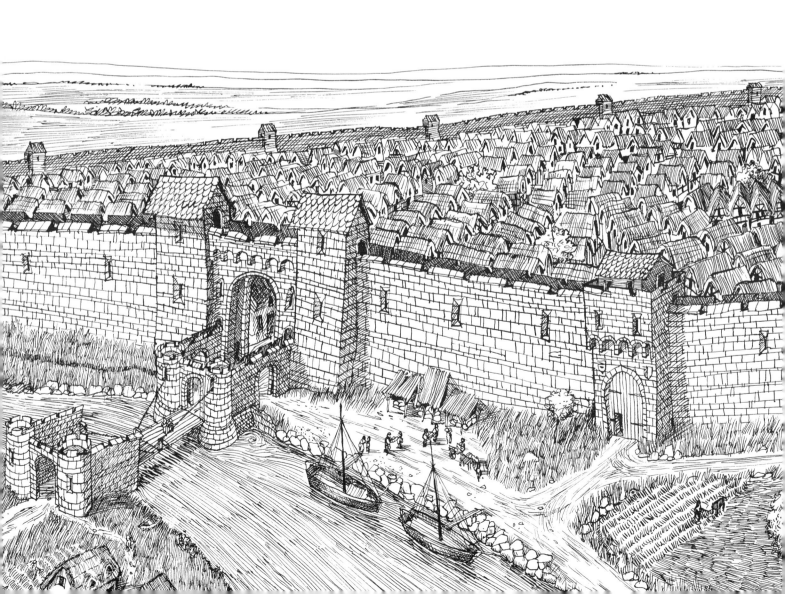

CATHEDRAL

The Story of Its Construction

DAVID MACAULAY

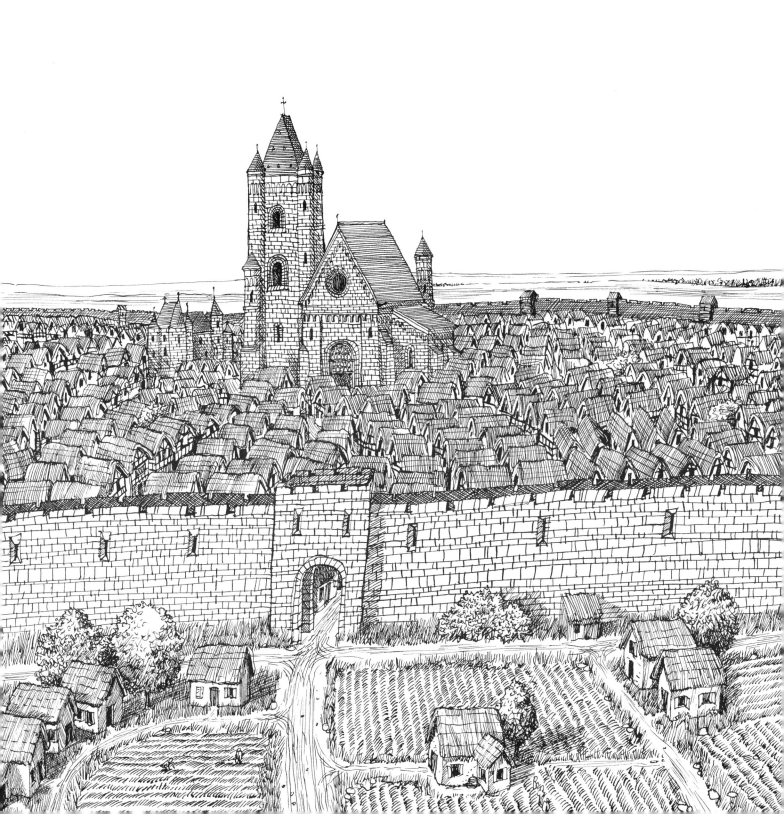

PREFACE

The cathedral of Chutreaux is imaginary, but the methods of its construction correspond closely to the actual construction of a Gothic cathedral. The story of its almost uninterrupted construction, however, represents a somewhat ideal situation. For owing to either financial or structural problems or both, the completion of many such undertakings was delayed for as long as two hundred years.

Although the people of Chutreaux are imaginary, their single-mindedness, their spirit, and their incredible courage are typical of the people of twelfth-, thirteenth-, and fourteenth-century Europe whose magnificent dreams still stand today.

for Janice

with special thanks
to Mary and Hardu

Library of Congress Cataloging in Publication Data

Macaulay, David.
    Cathedral: the story of its construction.

    1. Cathedrals. 2. Architecture, Gothic.
I. Title.
NA4830.M32   726'.6   73-6634
ISBN 0-395-17513-5

For hundreds of years the people of Europe were taught by the church that God was the most important force in their lives. If they prospered, they thanked God for His kindness. If they suffered, they begged for God's mercy, for surely God was punishing them.

In the thirteenth century God was good to the people of France and especially to the people of Chutreaux. They had no wars to fight and the plague was gone. The weather was good for the farmers so there was plenty of food to eat, and business was good for the city's merchants. For these blessings and to help insure that He would continue to favor them, the city of Chutreaux wished to thank God. The people began to dream of building Him a new cathedral.

A new cathedral would offer a worthy resting place for the sacred remains of Saint Germain, a knight of the First Crusade whose skull and forefinger had later been sent back from Constantinople by Louis IX. Such relics as these were worshipped by people throughout Europe. And a new cathedral was an attractive idea for yet another reason. At the time the people of nearby Amiens, Beauvais, and Rouen were building new cathedrals. The people of Chutreaux did not wish to be outdone, on earth or especially in heaven.

The final decision to build a new cathedral was made in the year 1252, after lightning struck and severely damaged the old cathedral. The people of Chutreaux wished to build the longest, widest, highest, and most beautiful cathedral in all of France. The new cathedral would be built to the glory of God and it mattered little that it might take more than one hundred years to construct it.

Although the bishop was the head of the church in Chutreaux, it was the group of clergymen known as the chapter who controlled the money. It was the chapter who hired the Flemish architect William of Planz. William had gained his knowledge of architecture and engineering by visiting and working on many cathedrals not only in France but also in England and Germany. His reputation as an excellent master builder had reached Chutreaux through the returning crusaders. So he was summoned by the chapter to design and supervise the construction of the new cathedral, and to hire the master craftsmen who would work under him.

The craftsmen were the master quarryman, the master stone cutter, the master sculptor, the master mortar maker, the master mason, the master carpenter, the master blacksmith, the master roofer, and the master glass maker.

Each master craftsman ran a workshop for his own particular trade. He had many apprentices or assistants who were learning the trade in hopes of one day becoming masters themselves. Most of the heavy work was done by laborers, men with no particular skill. Some came from Chutreaux, some from the surrounding countryside, and some were working their way back from the Crusades.

Pickaxe

Hammer

Chisel

Template

Lever

Measuring Stick

Saw

Dividers

Square

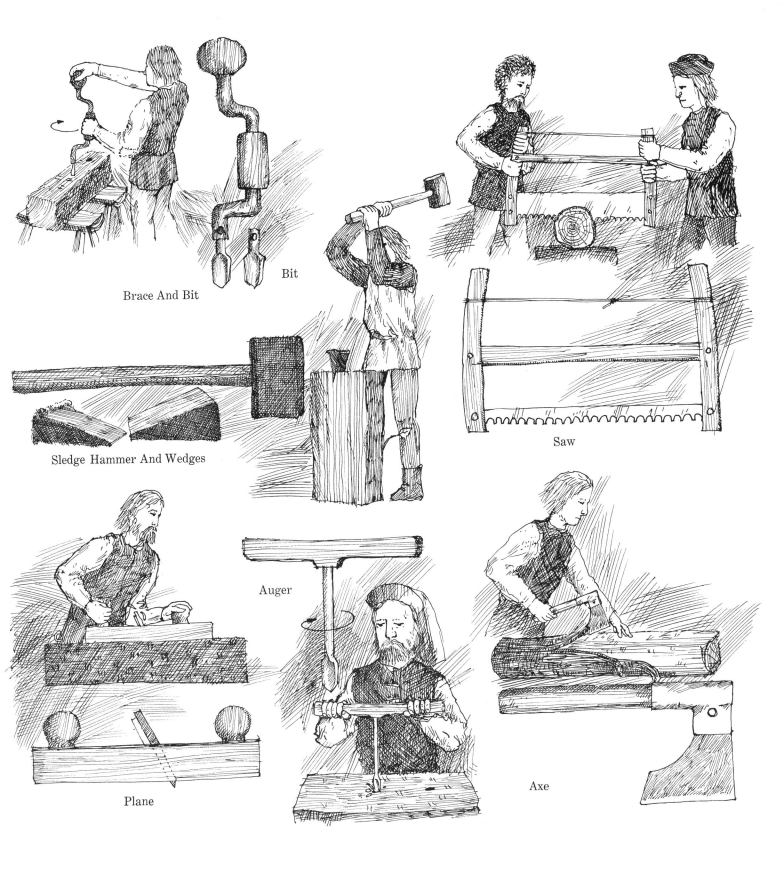

Brace And Bit

Bit

Sledge Hammer And Wedges

Saw

Auger

Plane

Axe

Each workshop required specific tools. All the metal tools were made by a blacksmith, and the wooden pieces were made by skilled woodworkers. The two main workshops, and those that required the most tools, were the stone cutters' workshop and the carpenters' workshop.

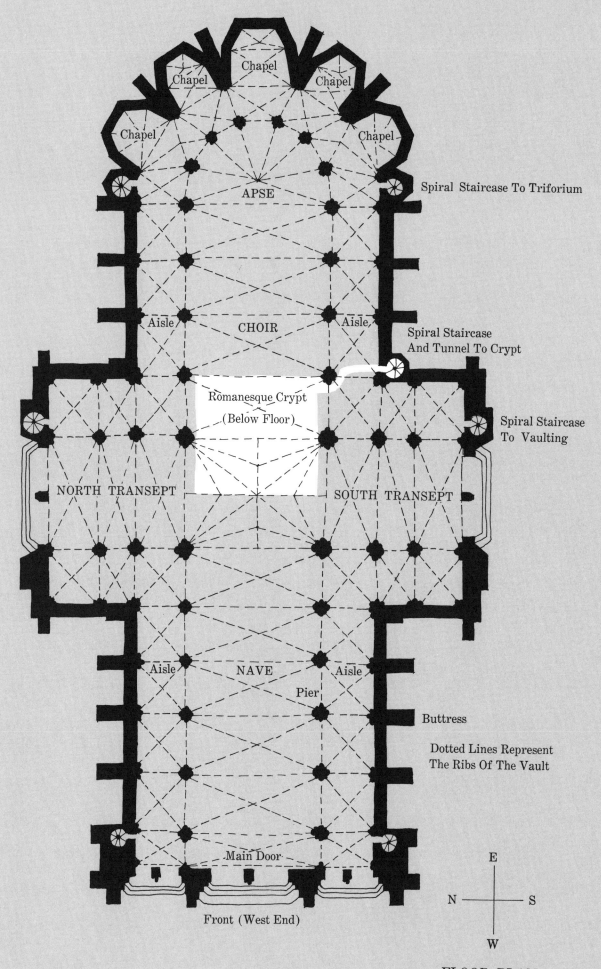

Chapel

Chapel

Chapel

Chapel

Chapel

APSE

Spiral Staircase To Triforium

Aisle

CHOIR

Aisle

Spiral Staircase
And Tunnel To Crypt

Romanesque Crypt

(Below Floor)

Spiral Staircase
To Vaulting

NORTH TRANSEPT

SOUTH TRANSEPT

Aisle

NAVE

Aisle

Pier

Buttress

Dotted Lines Represent
The Ribs Of The Vault

Main Door

E

N — S

Front (West End)

W

FLOOR PLAN

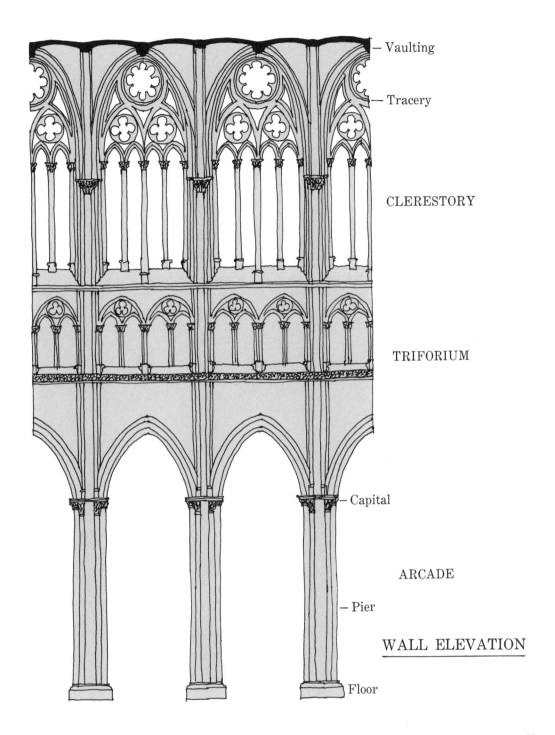

— Vaulting

— Tracery

CLERESTORY

TRIFORIUM

— Capital

ARCADE

— Pier

WALL ELEVATION

Floor

In the following weeks William planned and sketched and eventually settled on his final design. He combined methods and details from the cathedrals he had seen in his travels with his instruction from the chapter to design the longest, widest, highest, and most beautiful cathedral possible. The final designs were drawn on two sheets of plaster and presented to the bishop and the chapter. On one a floor plan was drawn that showed the layout of the cathedral naming all the different areas. The second had an elevation of one wall showing the different parts of the cathedral from the ground to the topmost vault.

Once the design had been approved, the master carpenter and his apprentices, along with one hundred and fifty laborers, were sent into the forest of Chantilly. Here the master carpenter supervised the cutting of timber for the construction of scaffolding, workshops, and machines.

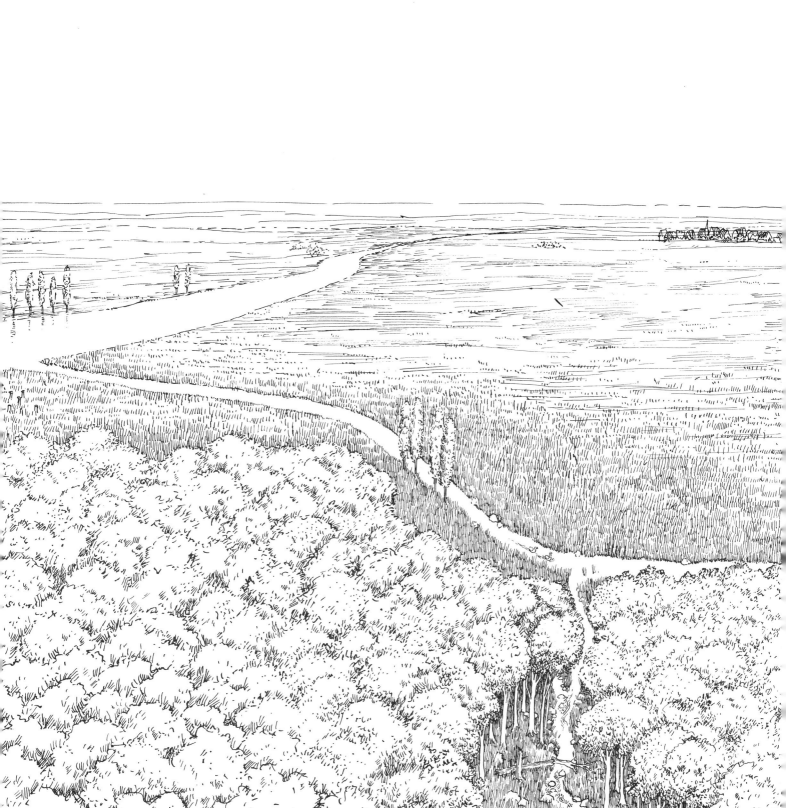

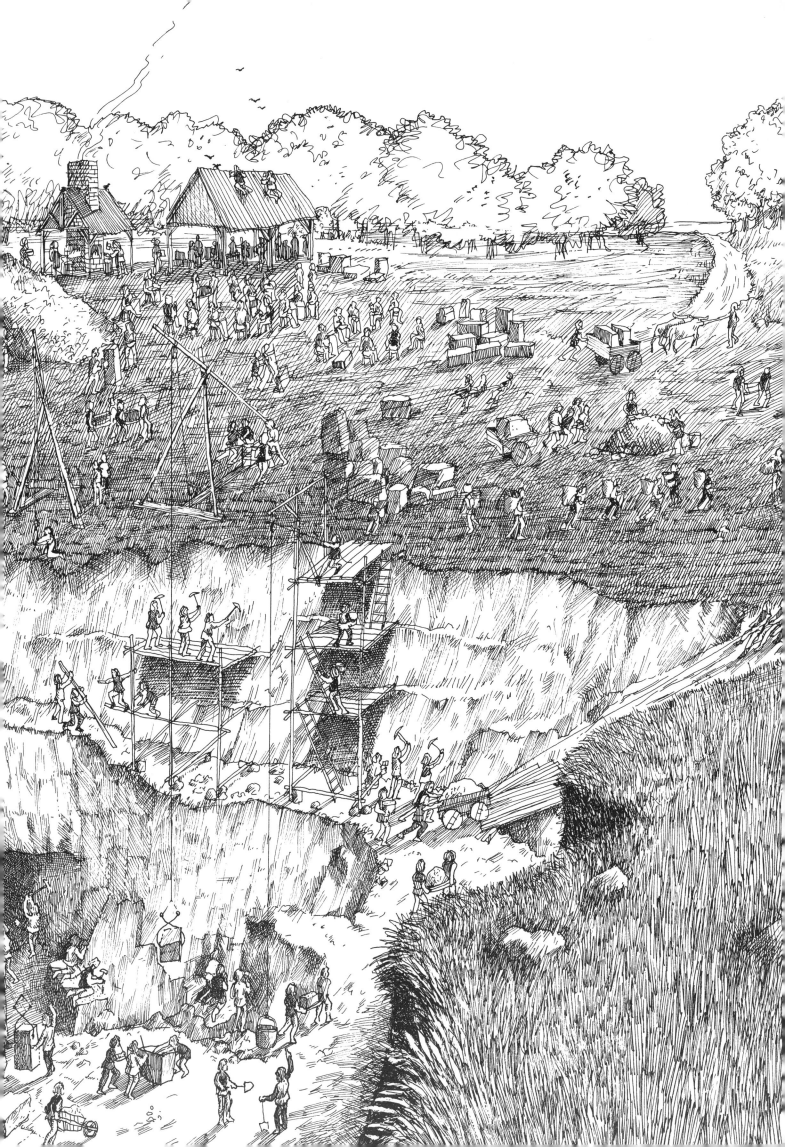

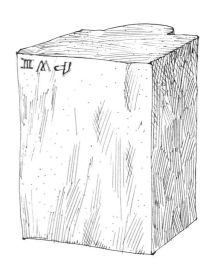

At the same time, the master quarryman was sent to supervise fifty apprentice stone cutters and two hundred and fifty laborers who would work in the Somme valley, an area known for its limestone.

A workshop was built for the stone cutters along with a forge, where the blacksmith could make new tools to replace the old ones as they wore out. Laborers helped the stone cutters lift large pieces of stone out of the quarry. Then the stone was cut, chiseled, and hammered by the stone cutters so it would match the patterns or templates supplied by the master mason. Each stone was marked three times, once to show its future location in the cathedral, once to show which quarry it came from — so that the quarry man would be paid for every stone he extracted — and once to show which stone cutter had actually cut the stone, so that he would be paid as well.

On May 24, 1252, laborers began clearing the actual site for the new cathedral. The ruins of the old cathedral were demolished except for the crypt, where the former bishops of Chutreaux lay buried. As the new cathedral was to be much larger, many houses were removed and even part of the bishop's palace was torn down. Once the east end of the site had been cleared, the location of the apse and choir was marked out with wooden stakes.

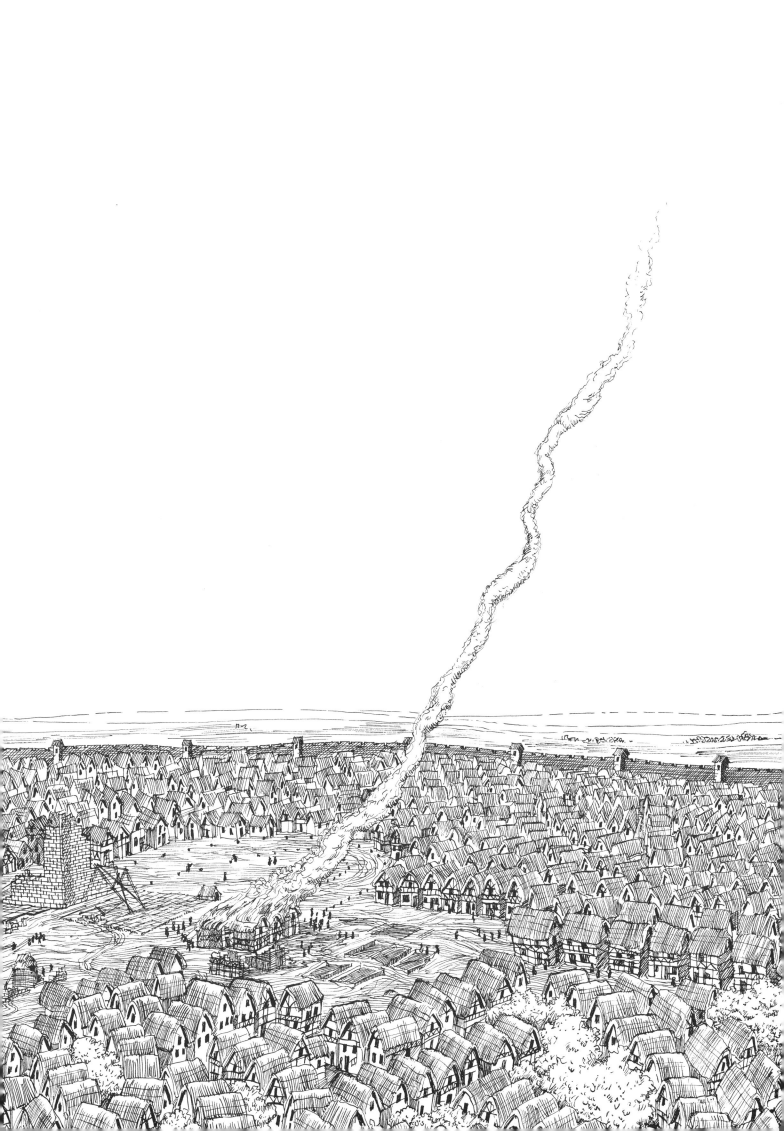

Workshops were built where the craftsmen could eat, rest, and work in bad weather. Another forge was built for the production of tools and nails. Finally the laborers began to dig the hole for the foundation. The foundation was to be made of thick walls, built twenty-five feet below ground level, which would support the building and prevent it from settling unevenly.

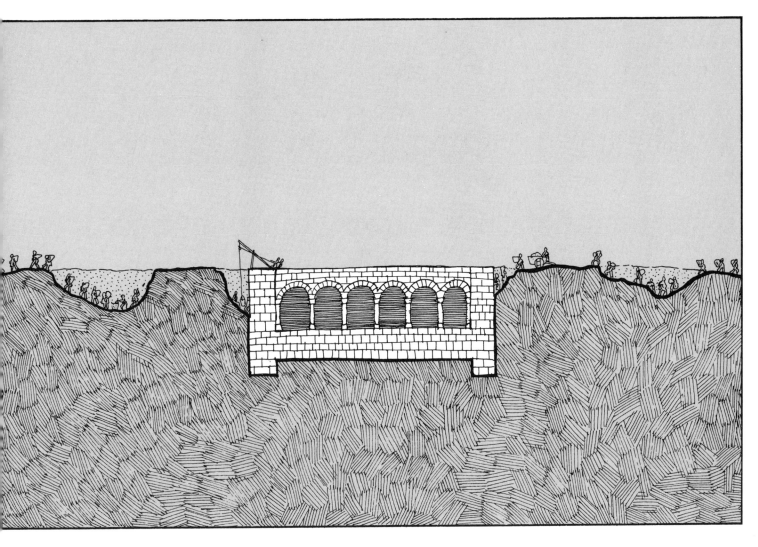

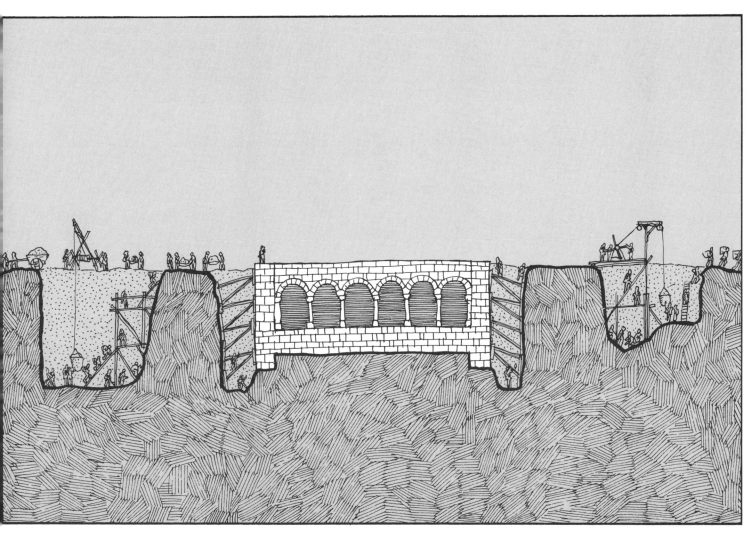

For the construction of the roof, large pieces of wood, some sixty feet long, had to be ordered from Scandinavia. Soon the wood and stone, which had been floated down the river from the quarry, began to arrive at the city's port. They were hoisted out of the boats with derricks and windlasses built by the carpenters and put into waiting carts that carried them through the town to the site.

By mid November the foundation hole for the apse and choir had been completely excavated.

On April 14, 1253, the bishop of Chutreaux blessed the first foundation stone as it was lowered onto the bed of small stones covering the clay at the bottom of the excavation.

The mortar men were ready with exact mixtures of sand, lime, and water. Laborers carried the mortar down the ladders to the masons who would lay the stones on top of each other, troweling a layer of mortar between each stone and each layer of stones. When it was dry the mortar would permanently bind the stones together.

The master mason checked continually with his level to make sure the stones were perfectly horizontal and with his plumb line to make sure that the wall was perfectly vertical. Any mistake in the foundation could endanger the wall that was to be built on top of it.

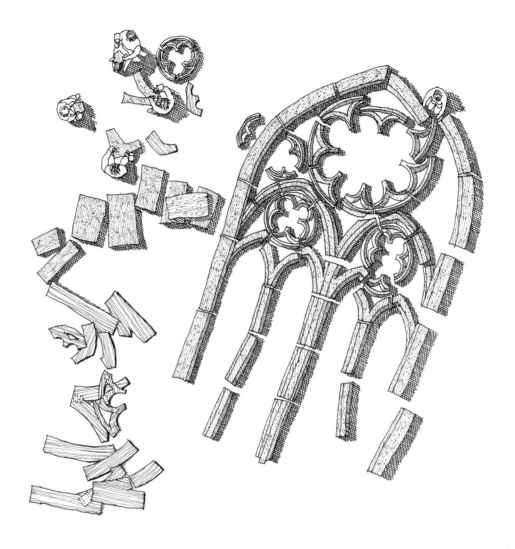

When the foundation was complete, work began on the walls. The walls of a Gothic cathedral like Chutreaux's consist of the piers or columns that support the vault and roof, and the space between the piers that is filled for the most part with the tracery — the stone framework of the windows — and small areas of solid-wall construction. The piers of the choir at Chutreaux were to be one hundred and sixty feet high and six to eight feet thick. They were constructed of hundreds of pieces of cut stone. The tracery, all of which was cut from templates, was cemented into place along with iron reinforcing bars as the piers were being built.

For the small areas of solid wall the stone mason would actually construct two parallel walls of cut stone. Then, using a piece of wood or chain as reinforcement, he would fill the space between them with concrete, a mixture of mortar and small stones. It would have been too expensive to build walls of solid stone.

The architect knew that buttresses had to be built to relieve the pressure the vault would place on the piers. These buttresses, erected on foundations next to the piers, would later be connected to the piers themselves by stone arches known as flying buttresses. In Gothic cathedrals the arched vault tended to push the piers outward. This force was transferred through the flying buttress to the buttress itself and then down to the foundation. In this way the main piers could remain quite thin in proportion to their height, allowing more space for the windows between them.

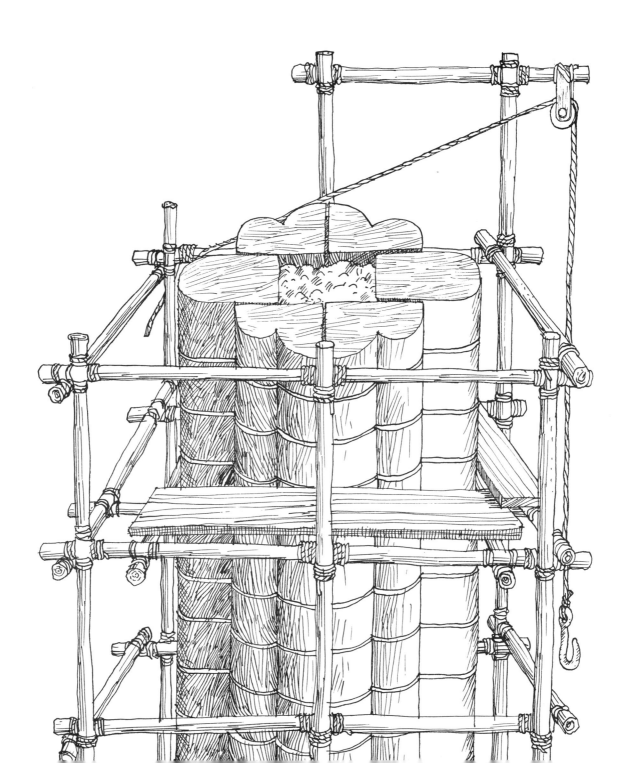

As the walls grew higher wooden scaffolding became a necessity. The scaffolding was made of poles lashed together with rope. Hoists were attached to it so that the stones and mortar could be lifted. The scaffolds also held work platforms for the masons made of mats of woven twigs. They were called hurdles and could be easily moved.

Since long pieces of wood were both difficult to find and expensive, the scaffolding for the walls above the arcade did not reach to the ground. It was hung from the walls and lifted as construction progressed. Ladders were not necessary to reach it, as several permanent spiral staircases were built into the wall itself.

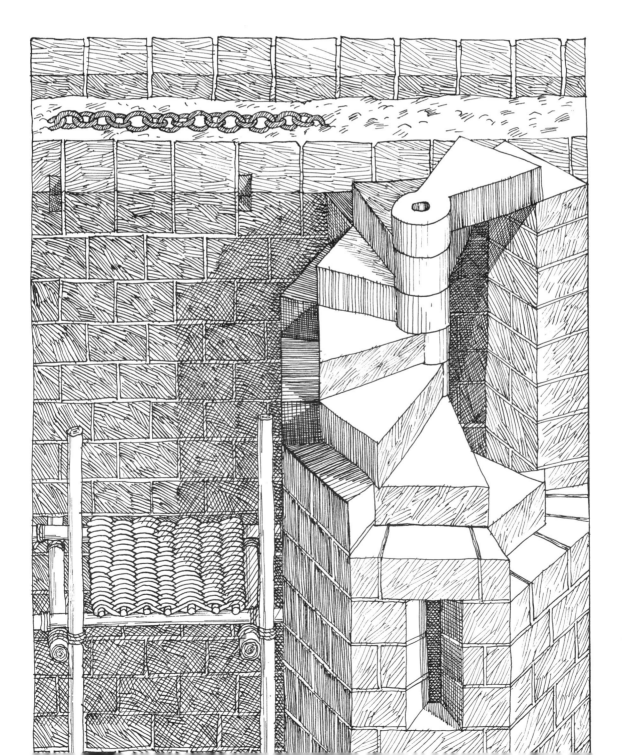

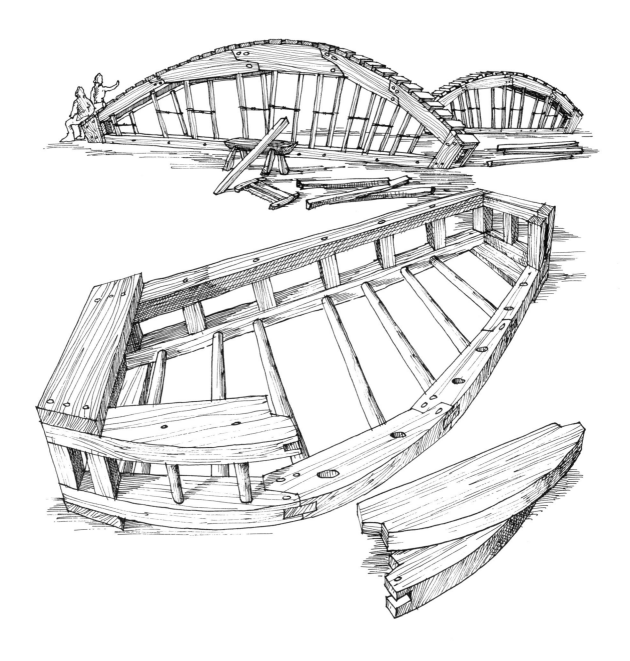

To build the flying buttresses it was first necessary to construct temporary wooden frames called centerings. These would support the weight of the stones and maintain the shape of the arch until the mortar was dry. These centerings were first built on the ground by the carpenters. Then they were hoisted into place and fastened to the pier at one end and to the buttress at the other. They acted as temporary flying buttresses until the stone arch was complete.

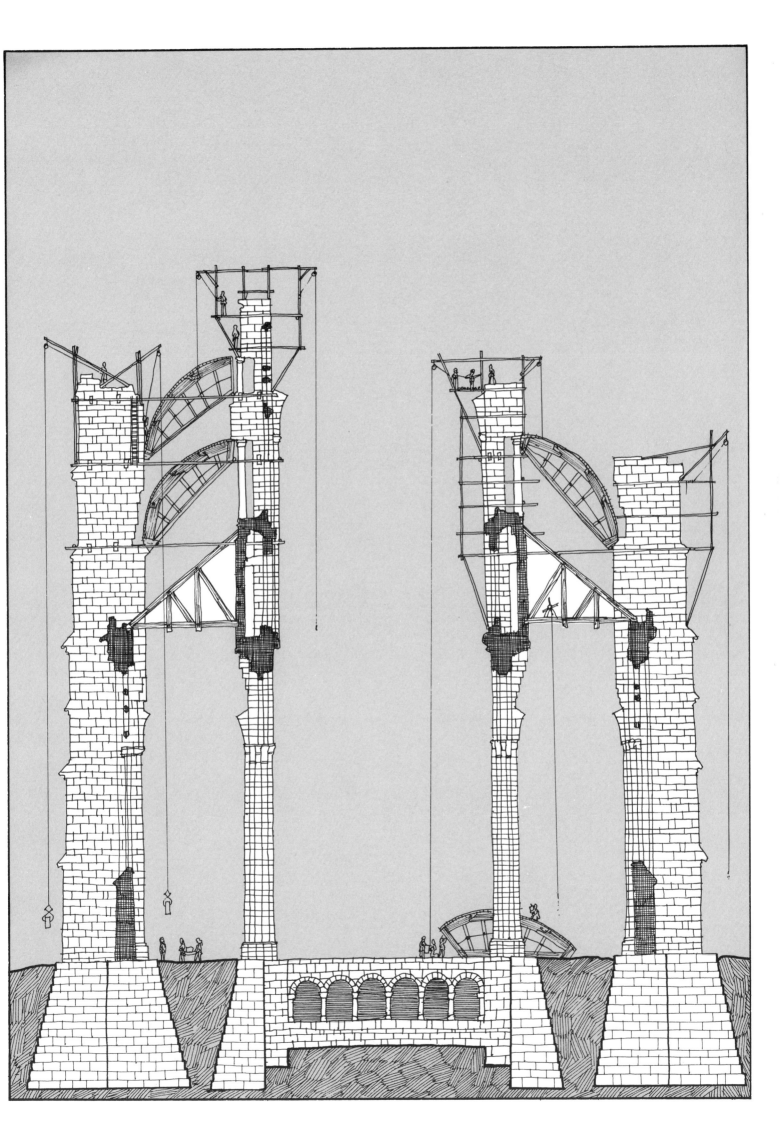

During the summer of 1270 the chapels in the apse and most of the piers and buttresses of the choir were finished. Much of the centering was also in place.

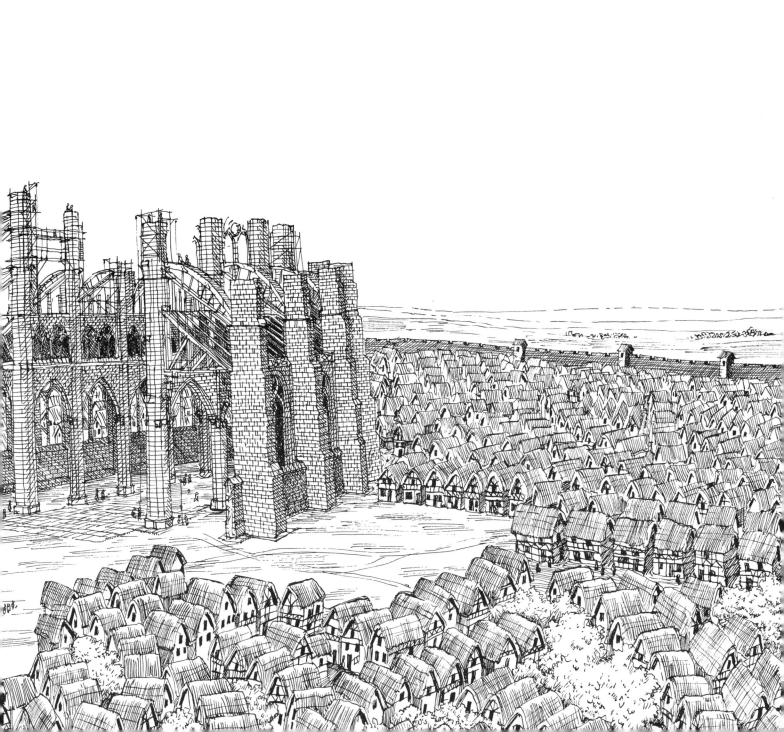

In November, as in every previous winter, the finished stonework was covered with straw and dung to prevent the frost from cracking the mortar before it had completely dried. Most of the masons went home for the winter because mortar work cannot be done in cold weather. Other work continued, however, for temporary workshops were built against the finished walls of the choir to house the stone cutters, who could no longer work outside. There they cut stones and tracery, carved capitals and sculptures in preparation for the return of the masons in the spring.

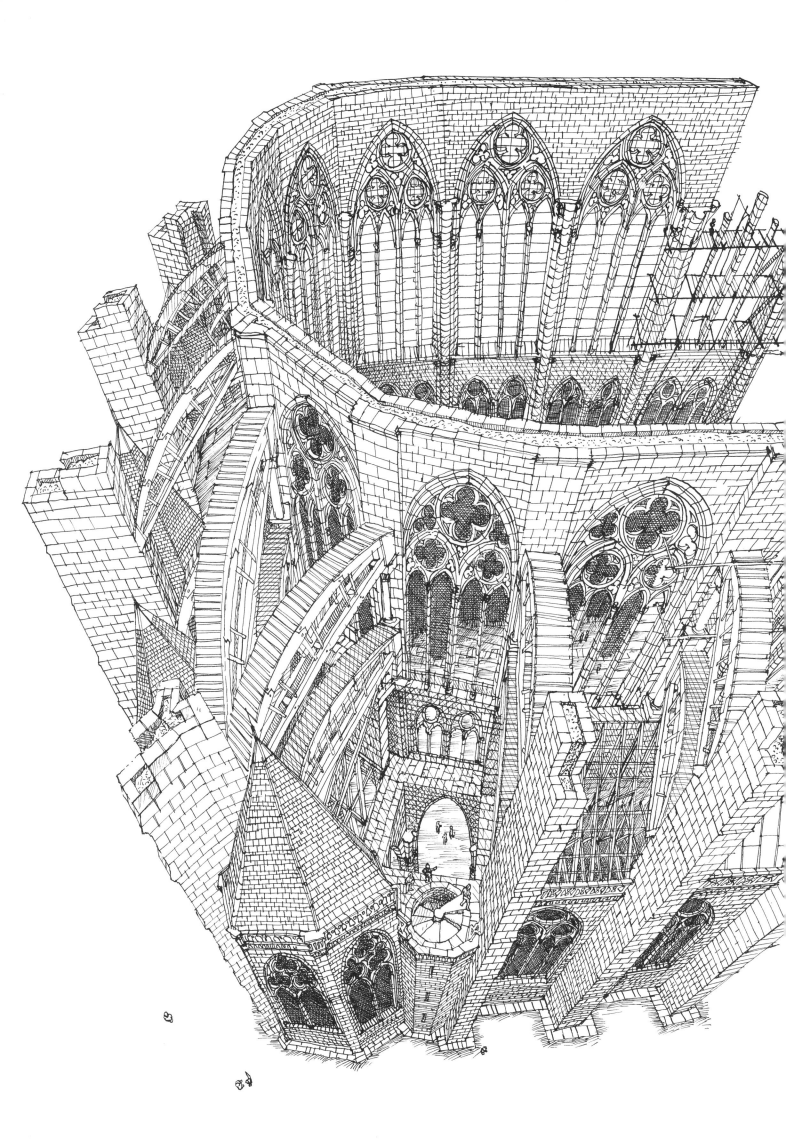

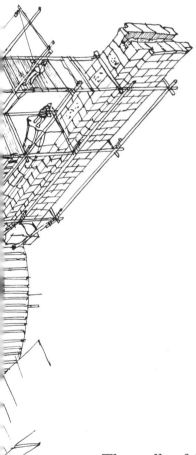

The walls of the choir were constructed in three stages. First was the arcade of piers that rose eighty feet from the foundation. Above them was the triforium, a row of arches that went up another twenty feet in front of a narrow passageway. And the last stage was the clerestory, which consisted of sixty-foot windows that reached right up to the roof.

Between 1270 and 1275 the walls of the choir and aisle were completed and work began on the roof.

The roof was made up of a series of triangular frames or trusses. The carpenters first assembled each individual truss on the ground. The timbers were fastened together by the mortice-and-tenon method; holes called mortices were cut, into which the tongues or tenons of other pieces would then fit. After test assembling every part the truss was dismantled and hoisted piece by piece to the top of the walls. There it was reassembled and the entire frame was locked together with oak pegs. Nails were not used by the carpenters in the construction of the roof frame.

The first few beams were hoisted to the tops of the walls using pulleys hung from the scaffolding.

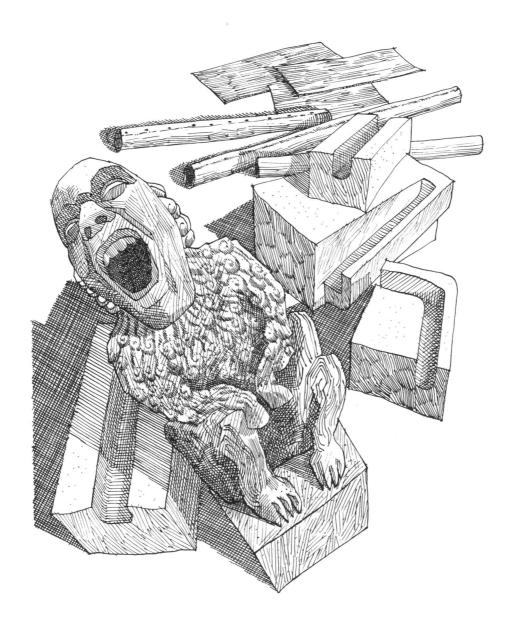

Once the beams were in place a windlass was set on top of them to hoist the rest of the timber and help in setting up the trusses.

Meanwhile, on the ground, the roofers were casting lead sheets that would cover the wooden frame, protecting it and the vaults from bad weather. They also cast the drain pipes and gutters. The stone cutters and sculptors carved the stone gutters and down spouts that were to be installed in the buttresses. These down spouts, through which the water from the roof fell to the ground, were carved to look like frightening creatures. They were called gargoyles and, when it rained, they would appear to be spitting water onto the ground below.

The gargoyles were installed on the buttresses and connected to the gutters at the base of the roof by a channel along the top of the flying buttresses. Then large vats of pitch were hoisted up to the roof and the timber was coated to prevent it from rotting. Finally, as the sheets of lead were nailed to the framework, the edges were rolled to prevent any water from seeping in.

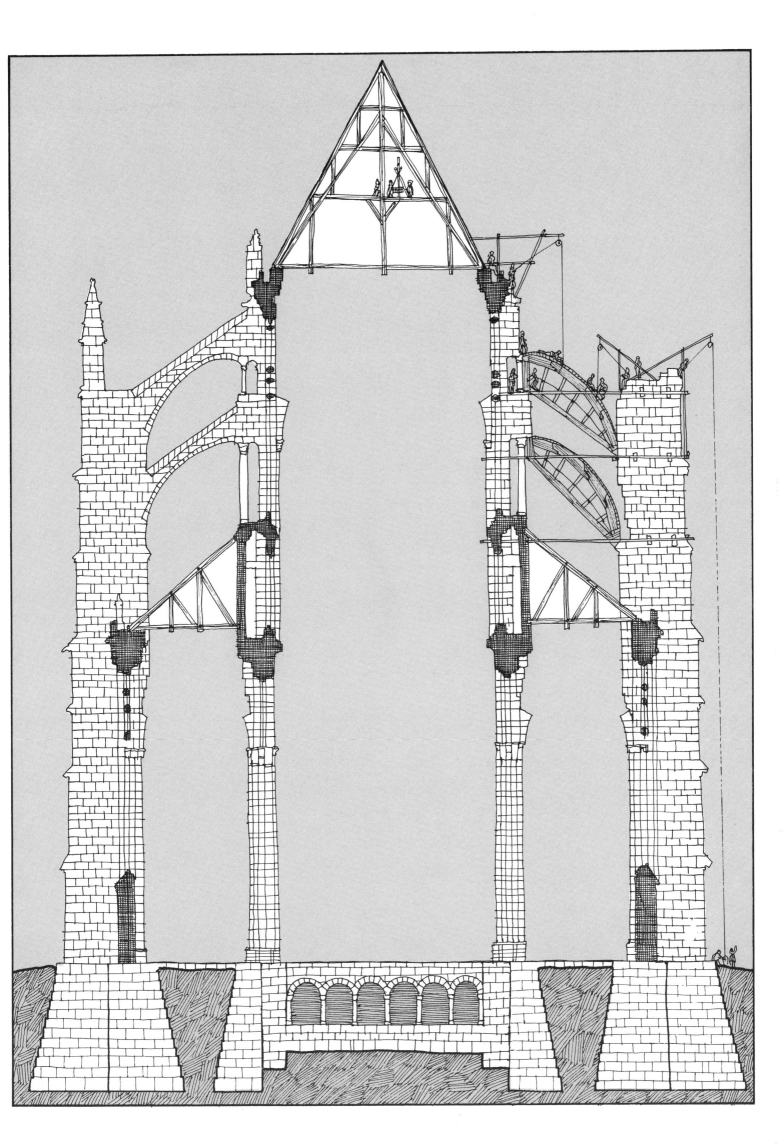

By 1280 the choir was ready for the construction of the vaulted ceiling and the foundation of the transept was begun. William, who was now too old to supervise the construction, was replaced by Robert of Cormont as master builder.

Two devices were used to lift the stones and concrete to the roof for the construction of the vaults. The first was the windlass and the second was the great wheel. The windlass, which had helped lift the timbers of the roof, was already in place and was used to raise the great wheel. The wheel was large enough so that one or two men could stand inside. Through its center ran a long axle to which the hoisting rope was fastened. As the men walked forward both the wheel and the axle turned, winding up the rope. This method enabled them to lift very heavy loads.

In order to construct the vaulted ceiling a wooden scaffold was erected connecting the two walls of the choir one hundred and thirty feet above ground. On the scaffolding wooden centerings like those used for the flying buttresses were installed. They would support the arched stone ribs until the mortar was dry, at which time the ribs could support themselves. The ribs carried the webbing, which was the ceiling itself. The vaults were constructed one bay at a time, a bay being the rectangular area between four piers.

It was during the construction of the scaffolding and centerings that the bishop of Chutreaux died. Work stopped for seven days. The bishop was buried on the fourteenth of September in 1281, twenty-eight years after construction had first begun. After a long service his body was placed in a new tomb in the old crypt. On the twenty-first of September Roland of Clermont was installed as the new bishop of Chutreaux.

When work resumed, the flying buttresses of the choir were completed and the centering was readied for the first stones of the vault.

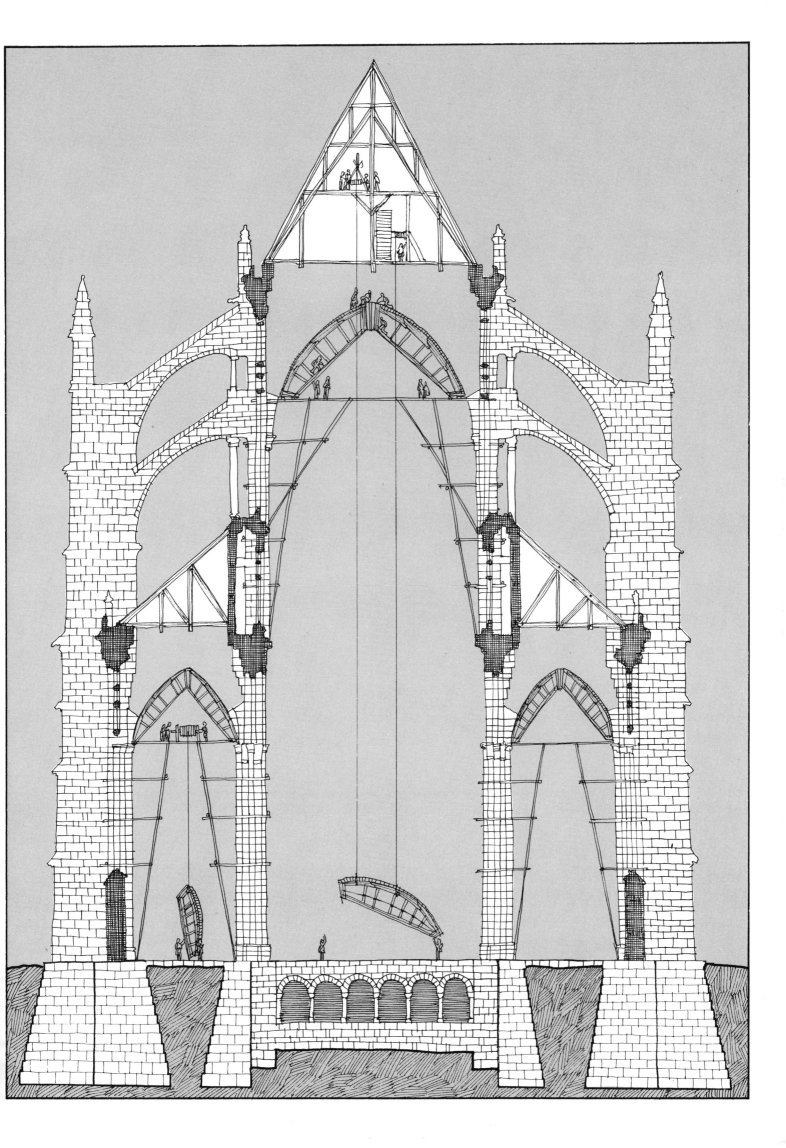

One by one the cut stones of the ribs, called voussoirs, were hoisted onto the centering and mortared into place by the masons. Finally the keystone was lowered into place to lock the ribs together at the crown, the highest point of the arch.

The carpenters then installed pieces of wood, called lagging, that spanned the space between two centerings. On top of the lagging the masons laid one course or layer of webbing stones. The lagging supported the course of webbing until the mortar was dry. The webbing was constructed of the lightest possible stone to lessen the weight on the ribs. Two teams, each with a mason and a carpenter, worked simultaneously from both sides of a vault — installing first the lagging and then the webbing. When they met in the center the vault was complete. The vaulting over the aisle was constructed in the same way and at the same time.

When the mortar in the webbing had set, a four-inch layer of concrete was poured over the entire vault to prevent any cracking between the stones. Once the concrete had set, the lagging was removed and the centering was lowered and moved onto the scaffolding of the next bay. The procedure was repeated until eventually the entire choir was vaulted.

By the first of May, 1302, the transept and most of its vaulting was complete. Since this was an annual holiday, instead of working everyone attended the May Day celebration and fair at the cathedral.

By this time the glass makers had started working on the beautiful colored glass for the huge windows. They made the glass from a mixture of beechwood ash and washed sand that was melted at high temperatures. After different kinds of metals were added to the molten mixture for color, the glass makers scooped up a ball of molten glass on the end of a hollow pipe and blew it up like a balloon. By cutting the end off the balloon and spinning the pipe quickly the glass opened up into a flat circular shape. It was then removed from the pipe and allowed to cool.

The glass was cut into a square shape with a grozing iron, a steel rod with a sharp point at one end, to the right shape and size for the window. The pattern for the window had been drawn on a whitewashed bench so that the glass could be cut to the exact size and shape simply by laying it over the pattern.

After several pieces of glass had been cut, they were joined by strips of lead. Single pieces of glass were usually no larger than eight inches by eight inches, but sections as large as thirty inches square could be made when held together by the lead. These sections were inserted between stone mullions and the reinforcing bars to create windows as high as sixty feet.

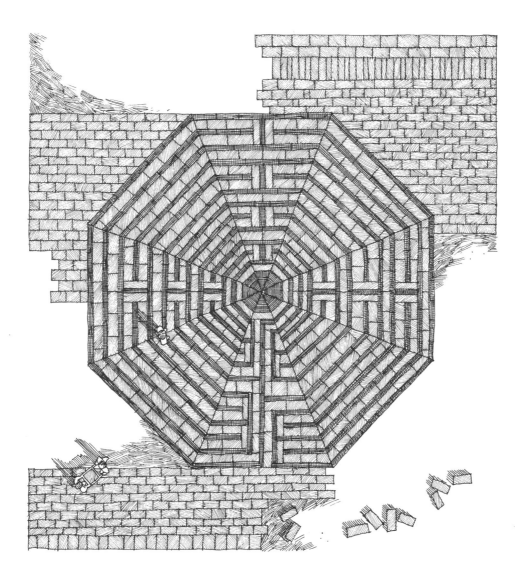

While the windows were being installed, plasterers covered the underside of the vault and painted red lines on it to give the impression that all the stones of the web were exactly the same size. They were eager for the web to appear perfect even if no one could see the lines from the ground.

Stone cutters and sculptors finished the moldings and capitals while masons laid the stone slabs that made up the floor. They created a maze pattern in the floor. Finding one's way to the center of the maze was considered as worthy of God's blessing as making the long pilgrimage through the countryside that so many had to make in order to worship in a cathedral such as Chutreaux's.

In 1306 work stopped again, this time because the chapter had run out of money. It was decided that the best way to raise the necessary funds was to exhibit the remains of Saint Germain. The people of northern France and southern England would gladly pay to see such relics, and so they were displayed for five years until enough money had been collected. It wasn't until 1330 that the nave was finally completed.

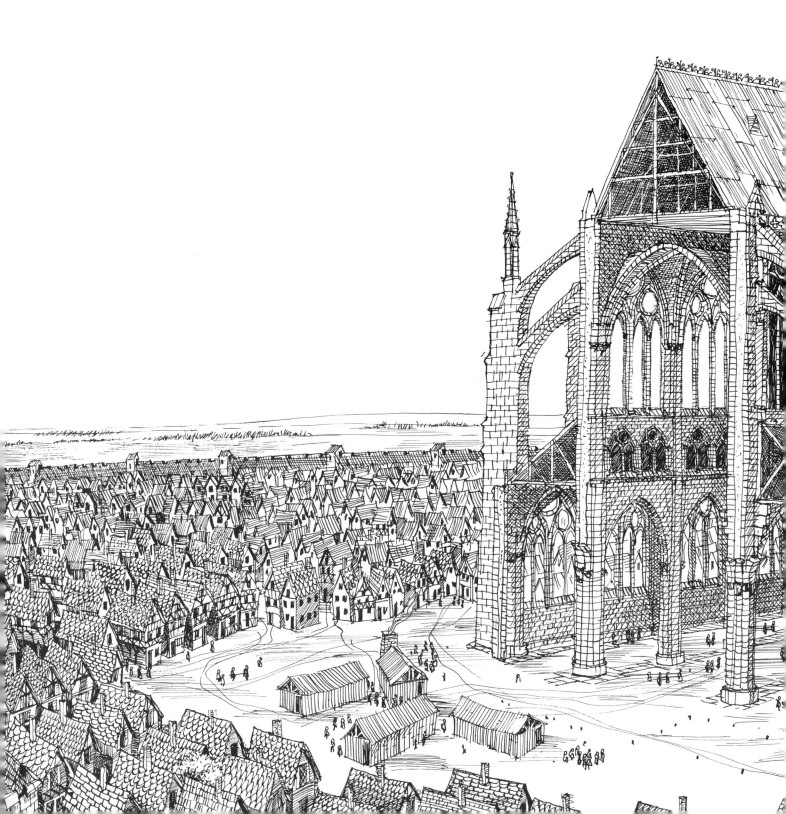

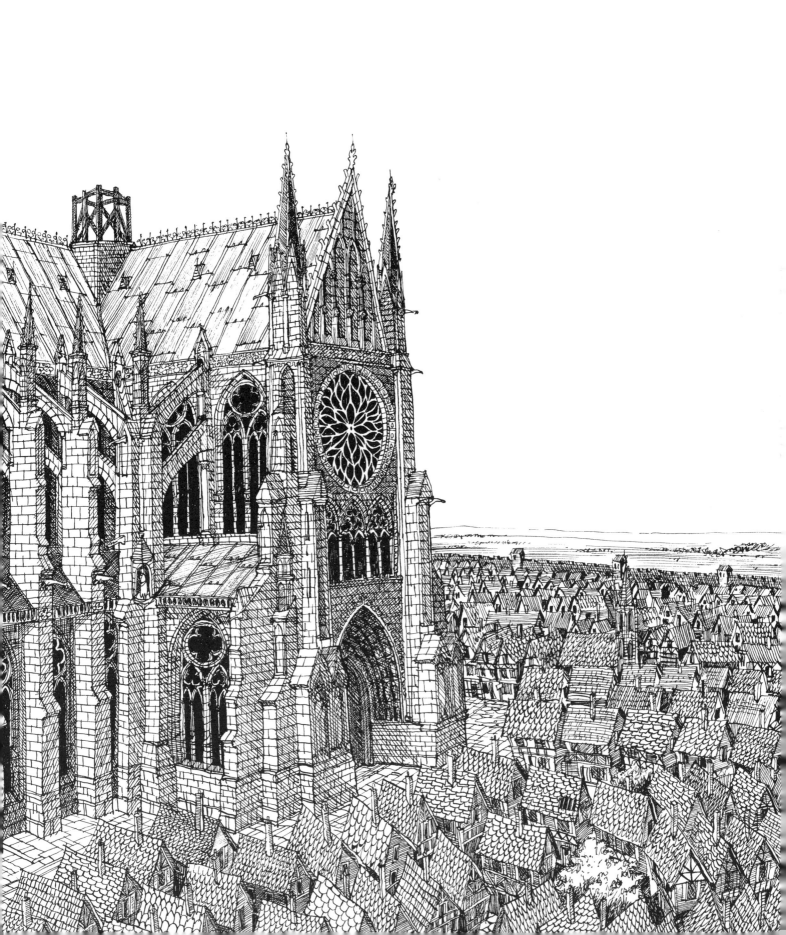

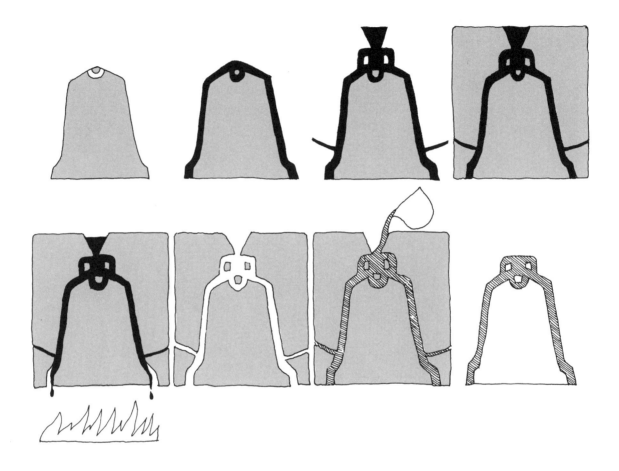

At the foundry in Chutreaux four large bells were cast in bronze. A model of the bell, as if it were solid, was first made of clay and plaster of Paris. It was covered then with a coat of wax of the same thickness that the finished bell was to be, and the required decoration on the outside of the bell was carved on the wax. This was then covered by a layer of clay and plaster compound.

When the whole construction was heated the wax melted and ran out, leaving a cavity between the outer shell and the core. This was the mold into which molten bronze was poured. When the metal cooled the mold was destroyed and the bell was prepared for shipment to the building.

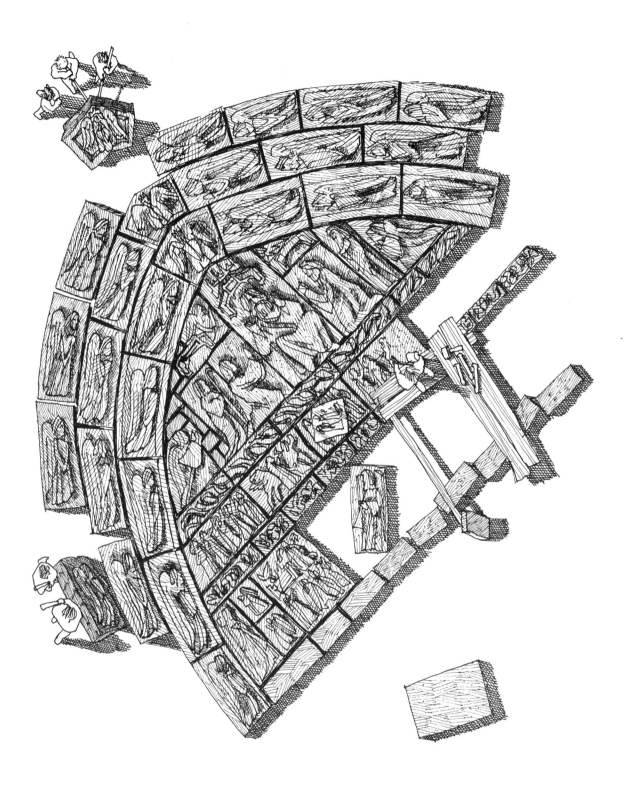

The tracery of the rose window for the front of the cathedral was carefully cut according to the plans. Voussoirs were carved to form the arched gables over each of the three front doors and a tympanum — a semicircular sculptured panel — was carved to go above each of the doors.

By 1331 the carpenters and roofers had completed work on the spire, which rose above the crossing of the nave and the transept. The spire was a wood frame structure covered with sheets of lead and highly decorated with sculptures and ornaments.

Meanwhile, in the carpenters' workshop the doors were being built. The center door alone was almost twenty-five feet high, made of heavy planks of wood and joined with cross-ribs. A blacksmith made all the nails for the door and a master metal worker made the bolts and locks and hinges.

In 1332 work was in progress on the west end or front of the cathedral. The construction of the towers was supervised by the master craftsman Etienne of Gaston. He had replaced Robert of Cormont, who died in 1329 after falling from the scaffolding of the vaults.

A heavy timber framework was constructed in the north tower. From it the bells were carefully hoisted and fastened into place. Four ropes hung down from the bells. When they were pulled the bells would rock back and forth, causing the hammers inside to hit the sides of the bells. The ringing could be heard for miles.

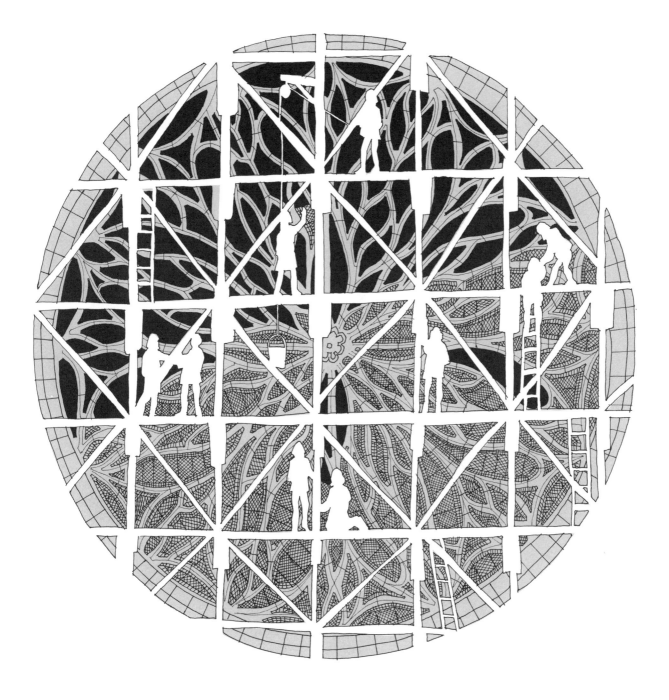

The masons put together the pieces of the rose window and installed the tympanums and voussoirs over the doors. Then the window makers came and filled the rose window's thirty-two-foot diameter with hundreds of pieces of colored glass.

By midsummer of 1338, the last pieces of sculpture had been hoisted into their niches. The cathedral was finished. On August 19 the bishop and the chapter led a great procession through the narrow streets of Chutreaux, returning to the grand, new cathedral with the entire population of the city for a service of thanksgiving.

Huge colored banners had been hung from the triforium and all the candles on the piers were lit. As the choir began to sing, the building filled with beautiful sounds and the people, most of them grandchildren of the men who had laid the foundation, were filled with tremendous awe and a great joy.

For eighty-six years the townspeople had shared one goal and it had at last been reached.

The people of Chutreaux had constructed the longest, widest, highest, and most beautiful cathedral in all of France.

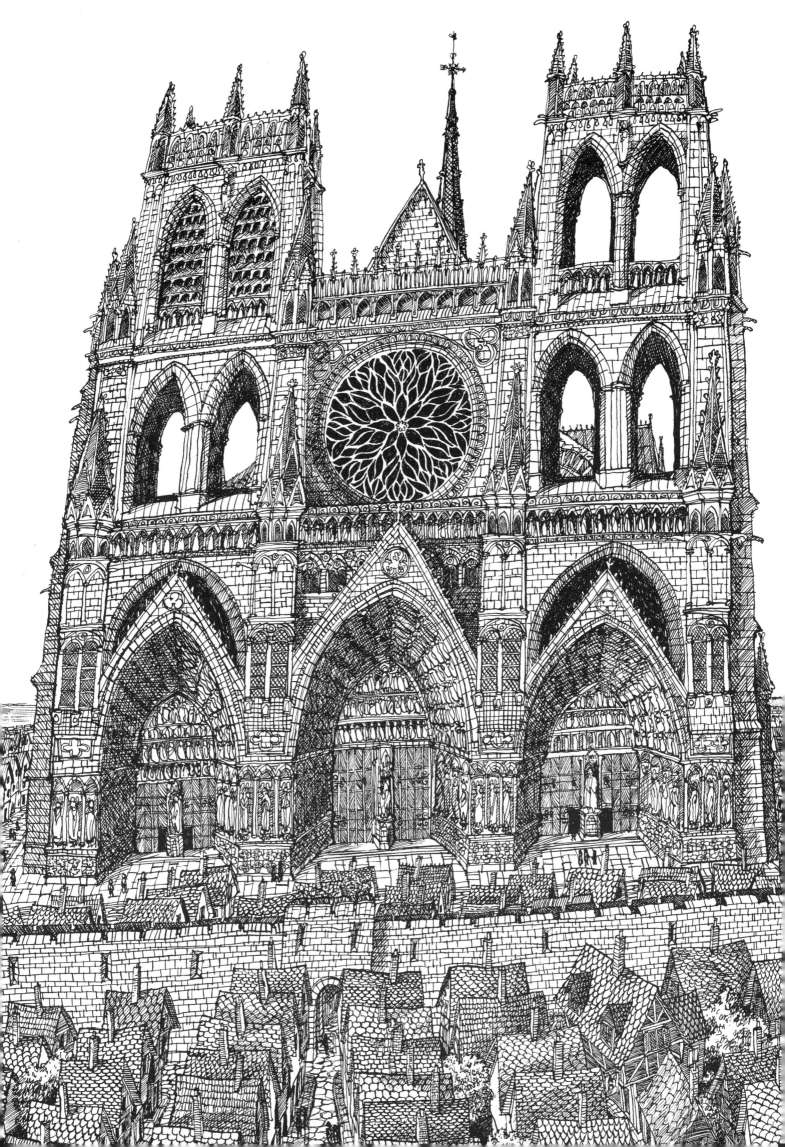

GLOSSARY

AISLE
The part of a church that runs parallel to the main areas — nave, choir, and transept — and is separated from them by an arcade.

APSE
The circular or angular end of a church, usually the east end.

BUTTRESS
Sometimes called a buttress pier, this is the large stone pier that rises across the aisle from the pier and is connected to the pier by a flying buttress.

CAPITAL
The form, usually of stone, that supplies the visual transition between the top of a column and whatever the column supports.

CATHEDRAL
A church of any size that contains the Cathedra or bishop's chair.

CENTERING
The timber framework that supports the stones of an arch until the mortar between them is dry.

CHOIR
The section of the church east of the transept that is sometimes raised above the level of the nave. It is called the choir because traditionally this is where the choir stands to sing during the service.

CLERESTORY
The topmost part of the church building whose windows illuminate the central portion of the interior space.

CROWN
The highest part of the arch, where the keystone is located.

CRYPT
A lower level, usually below ground, that is used for burial or as a chapel.

FLYING BUTTRESS
A stone arch that carries the thrust of the vault to the buttress.

GOTHIC ARCHITECTURE
The architectural style that developed in northern France and spread throughout Europe between 1150 and 1400. Large areas were covered by stone vaults supported on slender stone piers. By reducing the structure to piers the area between them could be and usually was filled with glass. The weight and pressure of the pointed vault is concentrated at the points where the vault touches the piers. This load is then split up. Some is carried down the pier to its foundation; the rest is carried across the flying buttress to the buttress and then down to its foundation. The most common features of Gothic architecture are the pointed arches and vaults, the large amounts of glass in the walls, and an overall feeling of great height.

HURDLES
A movable work platform made of woven twigs.

KEYSTONE
The central locking stone at the top of an arch.

LAGGING
Temporary wooden planks or frames used to support the courses or layers of webbing stone until the mortar is dry.

MORTICE AND TENON
A method of fastening one piece of wood to another. A mortice or square hole is cut into one piece of wood while a tenon or projection the same size as the hole is cut on the end of the other piece. The tenon is then tapped into the mortice, locking the two together without nails.

MULLION
The narrow upright stone pier used to divide the panels of glass in a window.

NAVE
The central area of a church where the congregation usually stands.

PIER
The pillar or column that supports an arch.

RIB
The stone arch that supports and strengthens the vault.

ROMANESQUE ARCHITECTURE
The architectural style that developed between the end of the Roman Empire and around 1000 A.D. In church architecture the nave became higher and narrower and the many columns that supported the triforium, clerestory, and roof were replaced by a few large piers. The flat wooden ceilings of the earlier churches, which kept burning down, were gradually replaced by round stone vaults. The round arch and the vault are the most common features of Romanesque buildings.

TEMPLATE
The full-size wooden pattern used by the stone cutter when he has to cut many pieces of stone the same size and shape.

TRACERY
The decorative carved stonework of a medieval church window.

TRANSEPT
In a Latin cross plan as at Chutreaux, the section that crosses the nave, usually separating the nave and the choir.

TRIFORIUM
The arcaded story between the nave arcade and the clerestory.

TRUSS
A triangular wooden frame. The roof frame is constructed of a series of trusses fastened together.

TYMPANUM
The sculptural area enclosed by the arch above the doors of a cathedral.

VAULT
The form of construction, usually of brick or stone, that is based on the shape of the arch. Used for the most part as a ceiling or roof.

VOUSSOIRS
Blocks of stone cut in wedge shapes to form an arch.

WINDLASS
A machine for hoisting or hauling. In the Middle Ages this consisted of a horizontal wooden barrel with a long rope fastened to it. The barrel was supported at both ends. When it was turned the rope would gradually be wound up around it.